Heaven Bound

Heaven Bound

CREATING A FUNERAL *or* MEMORIAL SERVICE
for YOUR PET

PARACLETE PRESS
BREWSTER, MASSACHUSETTS

Heaven Bound: Creating a Funeral or Memorial Service for Your Pet

2012 First Printing

ISBN 978-1-61261-244-7

Scripture references are taken from THE HOLY BIBLE, NEW INTERNATIONAL VERSION®, NIV® Copyright © 1973, 1978, 1984, 2011 by Biblica, Inc.™ Used by permission. All rights reserved worldwide.

Library of Congress Cataloging-in-Publication Data
Heaven bound : creating a funeral or memorial service for your pet / Paraclete Press.
   p. cm.
  ISBN 978-1-61261-244-7 (hard cover)
 1. Pet owners—Religious life. 2. Pets—Death—Religious aspects—Christianity.
3. Future life—Christianity. 4. Funeral rites and ceremonies. I. Paraclete Press.
  BV4596.A54H43 2012
  265'.9—dc23   2012014445

10 9 8 7 6 5 4 3 2 1

Published by Paraclete Press
Brewster, Massachusetts
www.paracletepress.com
Printed in the United States of America

This Book Is Dedicated to the Memory of

_____

Who Was With Us from

_____

We will love you always.

You enriched our lives.

We will see you again.

CONTENTS

How to Use this Book

A funeral or memorial service for your beloved pet is an opportunity to share memories, to laugh, to cry, and to record these feelings in the pages of this book. As you gather together with friends and family, tell stories about your family member who has died.

Don't worry about what others may think. Surround yourself with friends during this time.

It is good to grieve—and always helpful to share your grieving, as well as your joy, with others!

The relationships we have with our pets are just as complicated and special as those we have with our human family and friends.

There will be those who say, "It was just a pet." There will be others who remark, "You can always just buy another dog." Or cat, and so on. They don't understand. Not everyone will understand.

This is probably not the time to try and explain things to these friends or acquaintances. Instead, surround yourself with those who know about the friendship, companionship, and family that you have experienced with your pet.

Jesus said:

"Are not five sparrows sold for two pennies?
Yet not one of them is forgotten by God."
–LUKE 12:6

The relationships we experience with our pets can sometimes be among the deepest ones we will ever experience in our lives.

The sincerity, humility, dedication, purpose, courage, devotion, joy, and love that we have learned from our pets will stay with us forever. In fact, an animal companion can teach us about the love of God. As St. Paul writes in Romans 1:20: "For since the creation of the world God's invisible qualities—his eternal power and divine nature—have been clearly seen, being understood from what has been made, so that people are without excuse."

Our pets teach us Sincerity.

PSALM 5:3
In the morning, LORD, you hear my voice;
in the morning I lay my requests before you
and wait expectantly.

PSALM 37:7
Be still before the LORD and wait patiently for him.

Our pets teach us about Humility.

2 CHRONICLES 7:14–15

If my people, who are called by my name, will humble themselves
and pray and seek my face and turn from their wicked ways, then
I will hear from heaven, and I will forgive their sin and will heal
their land. Now my eyes will be open and my ears attentive
to the prayers offered in this place.

Our pets teach us Dedication.

1 CHRONICLES 16:11

Look to the LORD and his strength; seek his face always.

PSALM 145:18

The LORD is near to all who call on him,
to all who call on him in truth.

Our pets teach us to live with Purpose.

LUKE 18:1
Then Jesus told his disciples a parable to show them
that they should always pray and not give up.

Our pets show us the meaning of Courage.

PSALM 23:1–4
The LORD is my shepherd, I lack nothing.
He makes me lie down in green pastures,
he leads me beside quiet waters,
he refreshes my soul.
He guides me along the right paths
for his name's sake.
Even though I walk
through the darkest valley,
I will fear no evil,
for you are with me;
your rod and your staff,
they comfort me.

Our pets embody true Devotion.

ISAIAH 55:6
Seek the LORD while he may be found;
call on him while he is near.

MATTHEW 7:7–8
Ask and it will be given to you; seek and you will find;
knock and the door will be opened to you. For everyone who asks
receives; the one who seeks finds; and to the one who knocks,
the door will be opened.

From our pets, we learn Joy.

1 THESSALONIANS 5:16–18
Rejoice always, pray continually,
give thanks in all circumstances;
for this is God's will for you in Christ Jesus.

PROVERBS 17:22
A cheerful heart is good medicine,
but a crushed spirit dries up the bones.

And our pets teach us to Love.

1 JOHN 5:14–15
This is the confidence we have in approaching God:
that if we ask anything according to his will, he hears us.
And if we know that he hears us—whatever we ask—
we know that we have what we asked of him.

Planning a Memorial Service

If you live in a place that already has a pet funeral home, you may choose to make all of your arrangements through them. If you do not, many people will organize their own funerals and memorial services for their pets. Either way, you may want to follow these simple guidelines:

Arrange for a viewing area where friends and family may say goodbye.

Be present with your pet during this visitation time, and to receive friends and family.

Encourage everyone who comes to write in the pages of this book. This is the place to keep their funny stories, warm memories, and good wishes forever.

Add photos of your pet, too. Encourage others to bring photos of your pet that they may have taken on shared holidays, family events, or vacations.

Allow yourself to express your feelings and to be supported by others in this time of grief.

Find some special ways to honor the memory of your family member. Use *Heaven Bound* as your album and your scrapbook.

You may want to also encourage participants to post short videos on YouTube and Facebook and other places on the Web, too, where others can see them. This is a way for people to participate who were unable to make the journey to your pet's funeral or memorial service.

This is, of course, a sad time. God wants to hear from us at all times. God knows about our sadness. God knows that we mourn, and God comforts those who mourn.

Here are a few verses from the Bible to remember about mourning and sadness.

PSALM 25:1
In you, LORD my God,
I put my trust.

PSALM 55:17
Evening, morning and noon
I cry out in distress,
and he hears my voice.

More encouragement from the Bible about comfort in our time of mourning:

ROMANS 8:26

In the same way, the Spirit helps us in our weakness.
We do not know what we ought to pray for,
but the Spirit himself intercedes for us
through wordless groans.

PHILIPPIANS 4:6

Do not be anxious about anything, but in every situation,
by prayer and petition, with thanksgiving,
present your requests to God.

A Simple Order of Service

Here is a very simple outline of service that works beautifully. Then, on the following pages, you will see additional resources, texts, and ideas that may help you as you turn this simple order of service into one that honors the life and memory of your pet.

In Loving Memory of

_____
[your pet's name here]

Leader: The Lord be with you.

All: And also with you.

Leader: O Lord, how manifold are your works; in wisdom you have made them all.

All: The earth is full of your creatures; they look to you to give them their food in due season.

Leader: To God, who in every time and season cares for the earth and all its creatures,

All: Be glory and honor, now and forever!

PRAYER

Hymn: All Things Bright and Beautiful

Remembrances

THE BURIAL

Leader: The peace of the Lord be with you always!

All: And also with you!

Graveside Opening Words

We have gathered here today to express our love for our faithful friend and companion, [pet's name], as we lay [his/her] body to rest in this grave. We thank God, the Creator of all life, for the years we were privileged to enjoy our [use descriptive words] friend, and for the happy memories [s/he] gave to us. Each of us can recall some loveable way that [s/he] endeared [her/himself] to our hearts. Let's take a few moments now to recall some of those loveable traits that endeared [her/him] to us.

Remembrances

[Invite everyone to share a memory, if they choose to.]

[Once everyone who desires to, has had an opportunity to speak, the leader continues the service.]

All of these happy memories warm and fill our hearts. They will remain with us for many years to come. [Pet's name] has lived a full life and fulfilled God's purpose for him/her in this world. A blessed member of our family has died but is not forgotten.

We shared our laughter and our frustrations and our tears with [pet's name], our meals, our work, our vacations, and our lives. Now, with grateful hearts, we give [her/him] back to God, Who gave [her/him] to us for a while to love and cherish.

Rest in peace, little friend.

Before or after the Remembrances, you may choose to offer a Eulogy. If you do, here are some ideas of how to get started.

Sample Eulogy

Our Father in heaven, we thank You for all of creation, for flowers and fields and gardens, for friends and family, and especially for our faithful friend and constant companion, [pet's name].

Our beloved [pet's name], though unable to speak, told us in so many ways that we were loved by one of Your creation. He/she showed us some of Your joy, some of Your patience, some of Your faithfulness, and some of Your love. We are the better for having known him/her. It has been said that actions speak louder than words, and [pet's name] lived out that principle among us.

May we do likewise in our lives.

We have come here to say farewell to this true friend and loving member of our household. We thank You, Lord, for sending us this beloved companion. [Pet's name] will not be forgotten. We will see him/her again in heaven.

(And everyone says) Amen.

23

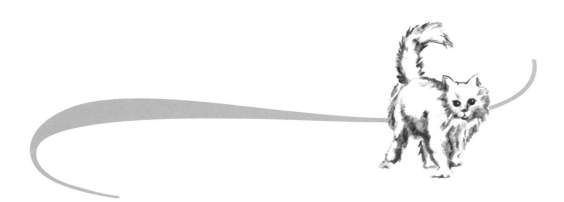

You may also choose to have a Scripture reading during your memorial service. This one can be ideal:

> The LORD God said, "It is not good for the man to be alone. I will make a helper suitable for him."
>
> Now the LORD God had formed out of the ground all the wild animals and all the birds in the sky. He brought them to the man to see what he would name them; and whatever the man called each living creature, that was its name. So the man gave names to all the livestock, the birds in the sky and all the wild animals.
>
> But for Adam no suitable helper was found.
> —GENESIS 2:18–20

Or this one:

"The Peaceable Kingdom"
a prophecy about a time to come

The wolf will live with the lamb,
  the leopard will lie down with the goat,
the calf and the lion and the yearling together,
  and a little child will lead them.
The cow will feed with the bear,
  their young will lie down together;
  and the lion will eat straw like the ox.
The infant will play near the cobra's den,
  and the young child will put its hand into the viper's nest.
They will neither harm nor destroy
  on all my holy mountain;
for the earth will be filled with the knowledge of the LORD
  as the waters cover the sea.
  —ISAIAH 11:6–9

Or this one:

> How many are your works, LORD!
> In wisdom you made them all;
> the earth is full of your creatures.
> There is the sea, vast and spacious,
> teeming with creatures beyond number—
> living things both large and small.
> There the ships go to and fro,
> and Leviathan, which you formed to frolic there.
>
> All creatures look to you
> to give them their food at the proper time.
> When you give it to them,
> they gather it up;
> when you open your hand,
> they are satisfied with good things.
> When you hide your face,
> they are terrified;
> when you take away their breath,
> they die and return to the dust.
> When you send your Spirit,
> they are created, and you renew the face of the ground.
>
> May the glory of the LORD endure forever;
> may the LORD rejoice in his works.
>
> —PSALM 104:24–31

After the Burial itself, you may select to offer additional prayers, or a Closing Prayer. Here are some ideas.

CLOSING PRAYERS

May God, who created the animals of this earth as a help to us, continue to protect and sustain us with the grace His blessing brings, now and forever.

Amen.

26   Let us pray.

Heavenly Father, we thank You for giving us [pet's name] to love and care for. Now that her/his life among us is over, we give her/him back to You, from Whom comes all life and breath.

We are grateful for her/his endearing traits, and for the ways she/he brought happiness into our home and laughter into our lives. Grant us pleasant memories of this dear friend who shared our family life and gave us happy years.

AMEN.

———————

Heavenly Father, by Your Word you created the heavens and the earth and all that is in them. In Your wisdom, You blessed the earth with creatures of every kind, giving them to us.

Now, we ask You, God, to send Your Holy Spirit upon us as we commit to the ground one of Your creatures who has lived among us for these years. We give You thanks for [pet's name] and for all she [he] has meant to each of us. Stretch out Your hand of favor upon her [him] and bless her [him] now in death as You did in life. We ask this through Jesus Christ our Lord.

AMEN.

Suggested Readings

The Animals' Eden

The Animals' Eden is a beautiful walled garden where our dogs go until their human companions can come and join them. This garden is full of lush lawns and green hedges, flower borders and shrubs, and beautiful meadows of wildflower—all for our pets to explore.

All the dogs who have passed into the Animals' Eden and are waiting for their special humans are free to do whatever they want. Because it is a heavenly place, foretold in the biblical vision of the Peaceable Kingdom, every animal loves every other. They live in this Eden together in harmony. Horses and ponies graze and gallop in the meadows. Dogs romp freely on the lawns and sniff in the shrubs. Cats lounge on the patios, basking in the sunshine, or take their ease in the dappled shade of the great oak trees. Birds are no longer caged, but fly freely in the trees, eating the plentiful fruits and berries. None ever feels hungry, but are provided with heavenly food if they wish, so long as they can eat without harming the others waiting alongside them. And no one is ever lonely.

There they wait in this Eden for us to come. For although the garden is a beautiful and happy place, there is nothing more joyful than a reunion between dear friends who have been apart too long.

—Anonymous

The Rainbow Bridge

There is a rainbow bridge connecting heaven and earth.

Just this side of the bridge is a land of meadows, hills, and valleys, all of it covered with lush green grass.

When one of our pets dies, he/she goes to this lovely place. There is always food and water and warm spring or cool autumn weather, full of flowers and colors. There, the old and frail animals are young once again. Those who are maimed are made whole once more. They play all day with each other, content and comfortable.

There is only one thing missing. They are not with the special people who loved them on earth. So each day they run and play until the day comes when one suddenly stops playing and looks up! Then, the nose twitches! The ears prick up! The eyes are focused intently! You have been seen, and suddenly, that one runs from the group.

You gather him/her up in your arms and embrace. Your face is kissed again and again and you look once more into the eyes of your trusting friend.

Then, together, you cross the rainbow bridge, a metaphor for the heaven that is to come, never again to be separated.

—ANONYMOUS

Perhaps your Memorial Service requires a bit of humor—or a warm touch. Here are a few options:

"No one appreciates the very special genius of your conversation
as the dog does."
—CHRISTOPHER MORLEY

"You think dogs will not be in heaven? I tell you, they will be there
long before any of us."
—ROBERT LOUIS STEVENSON

"What greater gift than the love of a cat?"
—CHARLES DICKENS

"If a dog will not come to you after having looked you in the face,
you should go home and examine your conscience."
—PRESIDENT WOODROW WILSON

"The great pleasure of a dog is that you may make a fool of yourself
with him and not only will he not scold you, but he will make a fool of
himself too."
—SAMUEL BUTLER

"One of the ways in which cats show happiness is by sleeping."
—CLEVELAND AMORY

"You ask of my companions. Hills, sir, and the sundown, and a dog as large as myself that my father bought me. They are better than human beings, because they know but do not tell."
—EMILY DICKINSON

Memories!

Memories!

$\overline{32}$

Memories!

33

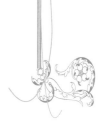

Memories!

Memories!

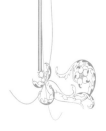

Memories!

Memories!

Memories!

Memories!

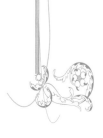

Memories!

Memories!

41

$\overline{42}$

Memories!

$$\overline{43}$$

Memories!

Memories!

$\overline{45}$

Memories!

$\overline{46}$

Memories!

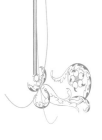

Memories!

48

Memories!

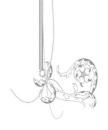

Memories!

$\overline{50}$

Memories!

$$\overline{51}$$

Memories!

Memories!

Memories!

Memories!

55

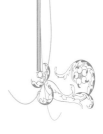

Memories!

Memories!

Memories!

Memories!

Additional Resources

THERE ARE MANY BOOKS, VIDEOS, WEBSITES, SUPPORT GROUPS, AND COUNSELING SERVICES FOR THOSE WHO HAVE HAD A BELOVED PET DIE.

ISBN:978-1-55725-732-1

ISBN:978-1-55725-959-2

This book—available in both dog and cat lover's editions—has helped many thousands of people. Friar Jack Wintz wants you to know: The Bible says we will be with our pets in heaven for eternity!

"Our God is a God of overflowing love, goodness, and beauty who is ready to give over everything to those he loves. This goodness is reflected in the whole family of creation. When God says of any creature, whether human or nonhuman, that it is good or very good, it's not simply a matter of moral goodness. The creature also has an inherent goodness and beauty— a beauty that reflects God, who is Beauty itself."

—FROM THE BOOK

Includes blessings and prayers.
Special presentation pages.

As a longtime editor of *St. Anthony Messenger* magazine, FRIAR JACK WINTZ, OFM, has interviewed many fascinating people, from Mother Teresa of Calcutta to Gene Kelly, Bob Newhart to Martin Sheen. He is a Franciscan friar, the author of the e-newsletter *Friar Jack's E-spirations* (www.friarjack.org), and lives in Cincinnati.

ISBN: 978-1-61261-161-7
Total running time: 31 minutes

For the first time, a video of support for those who grieve the loss of a beloved animal companion. Look for it in your local public library.

"Animals are guileless. That sort of honesty touches the human heart in a unique way. It allows us to see a better side of ourselves than sometimes is visible in our relationships with our fellow human beings."

—Brother Christopher Savage
(from *We Will Miss You*)

We learn love, faithfulness, and trust by living closely with our beloved animal companions. We invest a deep part of ourselves in the relationships we have with them. They are our family. When a beloved pet dies, we become vividly aware of the loss, and we need support that understands the depth of our love and attachment as well as the importance of the life of an animal. This video offers this level of support as you grieve the death of a pet who was a companion, a family member, and a friend.

Topics covered on *We Will Miss You* include these:

- The human-pet relationship is unique.
- Grief can be unexpected.
- You may experience feelings of guilt.
- Women, men, and children grieve differently.
- Other pets will also grieve.
- Some people will not understand.
- Create your own simple funeral or memorial.
- Consider whether to get another pet.
- Ritual is important.

INTERVIEWS: Br. Christopher Savage, New Skete Monastery, Cambridge, New York; Dr. Claire Sharp, DVM, Cummings School of Veterinary Medicine, Tufts University; Anne Lindsey, Founder, Massachusetts Animal Coalition

Other Paraclete DVDs for those who grieve:

ISBN: 978-1-55725-649-2   ISBN: 978-1-55725-998-1

Call 1-800-451-5006 or visit www.paracletepress.com for clips and more details.

FOR ADDITIONAL SUPPORT AS YOU GRIEVE THE DEATH OF A PET,
YOU MAY WANT TO CONTACT:

64

- CUMMINGS SCHOOL OF VETERINARY MEDICINE PET LOSS SUPPORT HOTLINE. The Pet Loss Support Hotline helps pet owners who have lost an animal companion. First- and second-year veterinary students, trained by a licensed psychologist, are available Monday through Friday from 6:00 PM to 9:00 PM at (508) 839-7966.
- PET LOSS GRIEF SUPPORT WEBSITE: www.petloss.com
- PET LOSS SUPPORT PAGE: www.pet-loss.net
- ASSOCIATION FOR PET LOSS AND BEREAVEMENT: www.aplb.org
- FINAL GIFT PET MEMORIAL CENTER: www.finalgift.com

About Paraclete Press

WHO WE ARE

Paraclete Press is a publisher of books, recordings, and videos on Christian spirituality. Our publishing represents a full expression of Christian belief and practice—from Catholic to Evangelical, from Protestant to Orthodox.

We are the publishing arm of the Community of Jesus, an ecumenical monastic community in the Benedictine tradition.

Learn more about us at our website:
www.paracletepress.com, or call us toll-free at 1-800-451-5006.